Praise for

Making Stone Soup

"In *Making Stone Soup* Jeff DeGraff once again brings deep and practical insight into how individuals and organizations innovate, why some teams succeed and others fail, and most importantly how you can improve yourself and your teams to create real innovation."

Dr. Peter Hortensius

Senior Vice President and Chief Technology Officer, Lenovo

"Jeff is one of the most engaging teachers, consultants and 'provocateurs' in the area of innovation. He packs his vast skills and experiences into this delightful new book. Moving seamlessly between concepts, stories and practices, Jeff offers a framework for innovation that is compelling, pragmatic yet visionary. It is a great read and a terrific guide for all of us who need to make 'stone soup' to innovate and grow!"

Raghu Krishnamoorthy

Vice President of Executive Development, Chief Learning Officer, Head GE Crotonville Global Leadership Institute at General Electric

"As a CEO in the knowledge economy, I've learned that collaboration is the key to innovation. Jeff DeGraff has been a fundamental influence on me and my company, *Big Think* to get us to understand and apply that learning. This book will help you do the same."

Victoria Montgomery Brown

Co-founder and CEO of Big Think

"The Dean of Innovation has done it again! *Making Stone Soup* is both engaging and powerful; it should be required reading for leaders looking to build innovation teams. Cutting-edge research, compelling stories, and practical tools are shared in a fun and thoughtful manner. Highly recommend."

Josh Linkner

Founder of E-Prize, New York Times Best Selling Author, and Columnist

ISBN-10: 0-692-24270-8
ISBN-13: 978-0-692-24270-4

The Dean of Innovation

Jeff DeGraff Innovation Library
601 E. University
Ann Arbor, MI 48104

Development Editor: Jimmy Farrell, www.targetmktng.com
Cover Designer: Maggie Chen
Book Designer: Miguel Trindade, www.targetmktng.com

MAKING STNE SOUP

by Jeff DeGraff

Acknowledgements

Very special thanks to...

Logan Scherer for his way with words

Miguel Trindade for his colorful creations

Jimmy Farrell for leading the way

Kenneth Gillett for making it all happen

Staney DeGraff for everything

Stirring the Pot

One of the first stories I ever learned to read was called Stone Soup. It was a tale about three clever soldiers with no food or money who come to a poor village and set a large iron cauldron by the well in the town square. As the townsfolk look on, the soldiers fill the vessel with water and ceremoniously place a large stone in the pot. Intrigued, the villagers come out to examine and critique the colorless concoction. Some suggest that the broth would be improved with carrots or potatoes and the like to which the tricksters agree. The meal gains momentum as the folks each willingly add some small ingredient. Soon the cauldron is bubbling with a sumptuous brew and all feast and dance in celebration. The story ends with the soldiers moving down the road to repeat the whole charade on the next unsuspecting burg.

I have never forgotten this parable about the generative power of communities engaged in small and diverse acts of creativity. At its most basic level, collaborative innovation is mostly about making stone soup. That is, getting everyone, everywhere, every day to make small unique contributions that when combined create something truly unique to be shared by all.

WHO
AM
I?

I have traveled around the globe speaking about innovation, met and consulted with the world's most powerful leaders and executives, but the biggest challenges I've faced and the greatest lessons I've learned have come from within myself. I speak from decades of experience: all of the approaches that you will find in this short book, *Making Stone Soup*, are all things that have worked for me. This comes from many, many years of learning from my early failures—from trying many different things and seeing what worked and what didn't work. The result is a set of real-life steps to achieving innovation in your organization and your life.

The stories I tell in this book are all very personal. I want to share with you both the highlights and lowlights, the thrilling successes and the instructive failures I've been through and reflected on as a consultant with dozens of top-shelf firms from Apple to Zappos. I've helped develop some of the biggest game-changing innovations of the past 20 years—including the largest clean energy initiative ever undertaken, the only best-selling soft drink introduced in the last decade, and the first on-demand video-streaming website to take viewers away from network television—and I've learned a lot along the way.

As both a professor at the Ross School of Business at the University of Michigan and a seasoned consultant to multi-national Fortune 500 companies, I bring to innovation both theory and practice. It's a combination of a carefully studied framework with practical, easy-to-follow action steps that will bring you and your organization to meaningful, long-term sustainable change.

Making Stone Soup is an interactive experience. It's about assembling a diverse group of thinkers and leaders and figuring out how to benefit from the respective strengths of each individual. Innovation is collaborative. It happens when people come together. In this spirit, I speak not as an expert but as a fellow learner. That's the other thing about innovation: it's never fully realized. There is no "there." If you've developed the miracle drug, there's always another miracle drug to make. If you've developed the great restaurant, there's always a second restaurant. We've never fully arrived—whenever we get where we think we wanted to get, there's a new place to reach.

I'm excited to see where we'll all go next.

CHAPTER 1

The Basic Ingredients

MAKE

STONE
SOUP

IMAGINE THIS:

inside yourself is a brilliant source of untapped talent, incredible potential. Innovation is a capability that you already have. To innovate is not to learn something new but to learn how to apply the power that you've always had in new ways and in new contexts. In the spirit of making the old new, let's start with an old but compelling metaphor: the making of stone soup.

It's a delicious concoction brewed from the unlikeliest of ingredients: bits of food that you wouldn't expect to mix together well.

It's a combination of ingredients that create a constructive conflict, or a positive tension, when you mix them. In this way, the ingredients are different, but they're not that different—they work well together. The idea is this: when people add disparate things together in small amounts, you get something new— something *special*.

Crucial to
the making of
stone soup is
collaboration.

This is precisely why
this old metaphor is newly
relevant in the world we live
in. We have entered an age of
all-encompassing social media:
collaboration at every level of our
lives. Bringing communities together
isn't just a skill—it's an imperative. It is
our way of life. Whether you are a small
business trying to grow with other small
businesses, or a non-profit museum, or an
educational institution—or even a grandmother
who wants to help her grandchildren find
meaningful employment—the key to jumpstarting
change is knowing how and where to connect with
other people.

Most people think that innovation is done only by geniuses who work alone.

Many more think that innovation is a hard, concrete object. This is simply not true. This book is about to demystify the way you think about innovation. Innovation is done by ordinary people who learn to work together. To innovate is not to invent something new. It is to find out how to do better what we can already do by joining forces with others whose strengths will fill in for our weaknesses.

We all have a dominant underlying logic to the way we think about things. Some people are big-picture thinkers. Others fixate on particulars. Some people are pragmatic and by-the-book when it comes to solving problems. Others are dreamers who go outside the box. Some people are goal-oriented, driven by the thrill of competition. Others are patient listeners, inspired by a co-operative community that they build around them.

We can become brilliant in our own dominant logic. The pragmatic thinkers are often excellent planners and organizers. The big-picture thinkers are dynamic energizers and experimenters. The goal-oriented thinkers are effective decision-makers and competitors. The patient thinkers are the best teachers and listeners.

But with our dominant logic also come blind spots—with every ability comes an inability, every strength a weakness.

Left by themselves, the pragmatic thinkers become bureaucrats. The big-picture thinkers become chaotic. The goal-oriented thinkers become control freaks. The patient thinkers become irrationally enthusiastic.

The key here is to know your blind spots and to use those blind spots—to know who and what can help you make up for the skills that your dominant logic may not necessarily give you. The goal is not to try to become a different kind of thinker but to embrace your dominant logic and learn how to complement it by surrounding yourself with thinkers of all kinds.

Innovation is not about alignment. It is about constructive conflict—positive tension. What happens when pragmatic thinkers work with big-picture thinkers? What happens when the goal-oriented thinkers meet the patient thinkers? This is exactly how and where innovation happens: you need to surround yourself with people who are not like you.

The Innovation Genome (iGenome) tells us exactly how and where these different types of thinking can work together to make growth happen. A strategic blueprint developed from over 25 years of academic research, the iGenome identifies the four different kinds of thinking—the four underlying logics that each represents a different approach to innovation: Create, Control, Collaborate, and Compete. What it shows us is not only how these different approaches work but how they work alongside each other, and how the tensions and harmonies among these four types of innovation can lead to growth.

Let's first look
closely at each of the
four colors of the iGenome,
and then we can begin to look
at how they interact with each
other. The goal is to understand
the tradeoffs and balances between
internal and external action,
and flexibility and stability
that happen when the four
iGenome colors work
together.

COLLABORATE
DO THINGS
THAT LAST

CREATE
DO NEW
THINGS

CONTROL
DO THINGS
RIGHT

COMPETE
DO THINGS
NOW

This quadrant is externally facing and highly flexible. This is the type of thinking that most people associate with innovation. What these people seek is radical innovation. They want organic growth—things not acquired but built. These people are revolutionaries. They are dreamers—expressive, clever, optimistic, charismatic, quick on their feet.

A prophetic vision is what carries a green workplace: stimulating projects, flexible hours, new initiatives, independent work streams. This is an environment driven by frenetic energy. Think Pixar. Think early Apple and late Apple. Think Vera Wang and Gianni Versace. Think Walt Disney and Steve Jobs. These are game-changers. This is the high-risk, high-reward profile. The crucial thing to remember here is that for everyone who makes it, there are hundreds more who fail. Taken too far, this prophetic vision becomes total chaos.

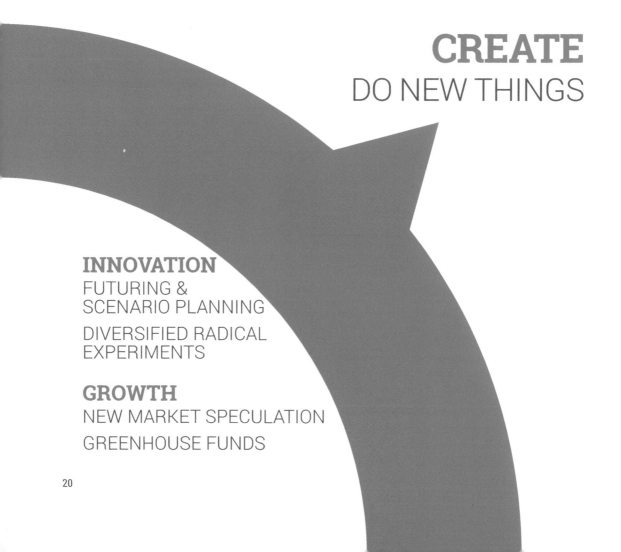

CREATE
DO NEW THINGS

INNOVATION
FUTURING &
SCENARIO PLANNING

DIVERSIFIED RADICAL
EXPERIMENTS

GROWTH
NEW MARKET SPECULATION

GREENHOUSE FUNDS

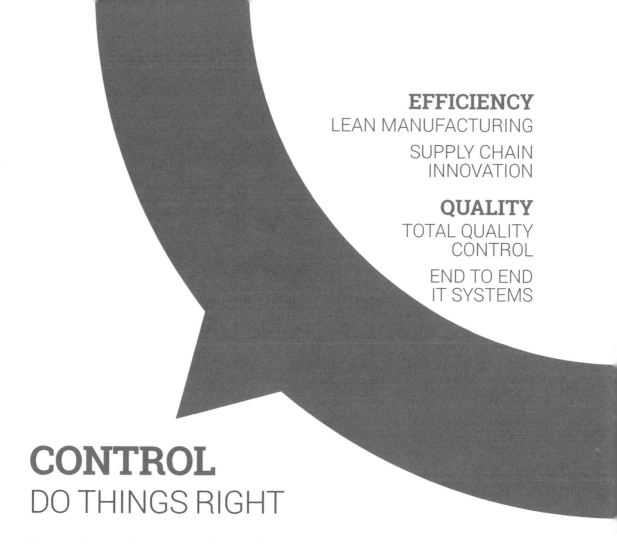

EFFICIENCY
LEAN MANUFACTURING

SUPPLY CHAIN
INNOVATION

QUALITY
TOTAL QUALITY
CONTROL

END TO END
IT SYSTEMS

CONTROL
DO THINGS RIGHT

This is the quadrant that pulls against the Create profile. If the visionaries of the green quadrant value experimentation and independence, the pragmatic thinkers in the red quadrant value order and structure. While the green profile creates deviance, the red profile eliminates it. In these workplaces, there are lots of procedures, lots of rules. These people are methodical, technical, by-the-book, objective, and persistent.

This is an incremental kind of innovation. For this reason, the innovation here is almost always low-risk. Since growth is driven by process, it is easily scalable. Think Dell Computer. Think McDonald's. Think Boeing and Toyota. Think British Petroleum. For these companies, failure is not an option. They are companies that make their money on scale. In these companies, you will always find complexity—there are many parts to manage. Taken too far, these pragmatic thinkers become control freaks.

It is a simple fact: the green innovators and the red innovators don't see eye-to-eye.

But they need each other to achieve growth. Left alone, green thinkers become orphans, who don't relate to the rest of the organization. Left alone, red thinkers become static bureaucrats. Green needs red to scale the business—to make the business replicable. Red needs green to help see the future. Without green, red will become habit-obsessed, perpetually looking backward. This is a productive tension—a conflict that is constructive. The goal here is to use the advantages of each quadrant at the right time: listen more to green thinkers in the early stages of growth, and as you get larger, listen more to the red thinkers.

This is the quadrant where we find the development of teams. These are the kind of thinkers who find the glue that holds a community together. They build an organization's culture—they tell us what makes us us. This is also the organization's fundamental source of knowledge—where the crucial competencies and capabilities are first developed. These thinkers are participative, patient listeners who gradually establish trust among the people they gather together. In these workplaces, there is a family atmosphere and a collaborative spirit.

These are people who are driven by their shared values—often by a desire to help others. Think Universities. Think Habitat for Humanity and Doctors Without Borders. This is a dynastic kind of innovation—a vision that gets passed down from generation to generation. The downside here is that this kind of growth is very slow. Sometimes it even takes a generation to develop—but once you build it, it is sustainable.

COLLABORATE
DO THINGS THAT LAST

COMMUNITY
COLLABORATIVE
COMMUNITIES
OF PRACTICE

CULTURE & COMPETENCY
DEVELOPMENT

KNOWLEDGE
KNOWLEDGE MANAGEMENT
SEARCH & REAPPLY

SPEED
MERGERS AND ACQUISITIONS

RAPID ACTION PROBLEM
SOLVING TEAMS

PROFIT
REVENUE INSIGHT
PROCESSES

MARKET
ADJACENCIES

COMPETE
DO THINGS NOW

This is the world of winners and losers, where the competitive spirit of laissez-faire capitalism rules. These are thinkers who are driven by profit and speed. They are masters at image-enhancement and deal-making. They thrive in high-pressure environments with quantifiable results.

Think Microsoft. Think Goldman Sachs. Think General Electric. These are companies that will produce revenue under any and all circumstances. The downside, however, is that this kind of fast-paced competition is the least sustainable growth of all the four quadrants. These thinkers do not have a long-term view—they do not have a vision for the future. This is precisely the opposite of the yellow quadrant.

At a larger level, the tension between the yellow and blue quadrants represents a generational conflict.

Baby Boomers are often blue thinkers—cutthroat, competitive, revenue-obsessed—while Millenials are often yellow thinkers—hopeful, slow-moving, driven by values. These are people who need each other. Without blue thinkers, yellow thinkers become victims of groupthink and irrational enthusiasm. Without yellow thinkers, blue thinkers have no vision of a future.

The goal here is not merely to understand your own dominant logic but to be able to rise above it. Innovation is not about you or any single individual—it's about you in the world. It is not about being a so-called balanced person. It is about embracing the strengths and weaknesses you have now and learning how to complement them with the strengths and weaknesses of the other people in your life.

STACK THE RUSSIAN NESTING DOLLS

Imagine your world as a matryoshka doll—a Russian nesting doll

You are the smallest doll. You—the individual doll—are contained within the next-largest doll: the communal doll. This is your friends, your family, your co-workers—the circle of people who make up your everyday support system. The communal doll is contained within the largest of the dolls, the universal doll. This is the doll that contains all of us. This is the outside world and all of the factors that may or may not affect our lives: the market, trends, diseases, political events, natural disasters. These dolls are both constraints and resources. Once we become acutely aware of these factors, we can use them to our benefit.

The key to becoming aware of all three dolls is to look in three places. Look up: follow the news—know what's going on in the world around you. Look down: ask yourself what you want. Look around: think about what your family wants, what the important people in your life want.

Innovation
is mostly just
connecting the dots,
building the community of
people and resources who will fill in
the gaps of your dominant logic. Innovation
is not about making new things but about
making things better, faster, and more efficient. The key
action here is to creativize. To creativize is not to create new
things but to take ordinary things and activities and to add
creativity to them. Once you build your innovation
community, you can take the steps to creativize
your world: set high-quality targets, enlist
deep and diverse domain expertise,
take multiple shots on goal,
and learn from experience
and experiments.

CREATIVIZE PROCESS
MACRO VIEW

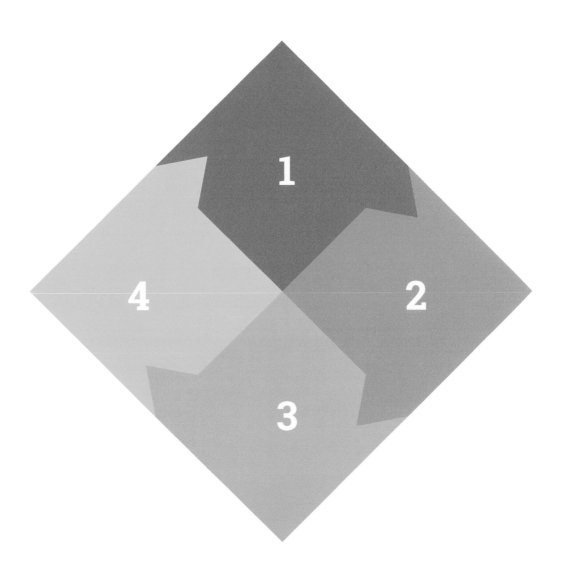

1 SET HIGH QUALITY TARGET
2 ENLIST DEEP & DIVERSE DOMAIN EXPERTISE
3 TAKE MULTIPLE SHOTS ON GOAL
4 LEARN FROM EXPERIENCE & EXPERIMENTS

CHAPTER 2

Set high-quality targets

In a world that's as noisy, hectic, and irregular as our own, it's not enough to have a vision.

YOU NEED TO SEE THE FUTURE WITH

RE-

VISION

Innovators are revisers. They change their minds. They're flexible. They adapt. In this revisionary spirit, stating your goals is only half the process of starting innovation.

The other half is re-stating your goals.

After you state your initial target, you will pay attention to the factors that surround it—the events and people in the world around you that affect that target. Then, you will have a deeper, more global understanding of this target and you can re-state the target in more effective terms.

Consider, for example, my own experience with stating and re-stating targets when I was brought in by a highly regarded medical school to assist in cutting down the time it took between performing a surgery and discharging the patient. At the time, open heart surgery patients had an in-house recovery time of about 18 days before being discharged, and this lengthy period of time was eating up money, space, and causing a great deal of stress for doctors, patients, and families. First, I asked to be paired with a medical expert since I had no medical training. The school obliged by providing me with one of the most well-respected and knowledgeable individuals in the field. Together, we began tackling the problem by looking at other medical institutions that already had a shorter period of time between surgery and discharge. We looked at foreign and domestic institutions and studied what made them successful.

While my partner and I were considering all of these outside trends and external forces influencing this issue, we realized that our challenge was actually a different, but pressing one. It turns out that the medical institution that we were working with, though extremely prestigious, was a pretty small fish in the pond it called home. Its size meant that it had little negotiating power in the medical community it was built in. Without that negotiating power, they would lose a considerable amount of money and have a great deal of trouble standing on their own as health care costs continue to rise. After extensive research and analysis, my partner and I had a new goal in mind: to pair this institution with one of the largest medical centers in the United States. Each side had a unique competitive advantage that the other did not and combining the two was sure to create a very powerful medical empire in the country's most powerful city.

Things were moving along with this merger; my partner and I had succeeded in getting all of the doctors to work together (not the easiest of feats) and we managed to successfully decrease the time of in-house major surgery recovery from 18 days to 8 while sustaining the highest level of care. Additionally, the competition between the institutions caused healthcare benefits to increase around the city. In this case, we benefited from re-thinking our initial goal by taking into consideration the various trends and forces at play in the medical community and realizing that a merger was the most sensible way of approaching this challenge.

We remained open-minded. We adapted. We didn't wait for the future—rather, we changed our ways as we felt our way to the future.

Let's start by stating your initial target.

The best targets are simple but powerful. They are specific and have an end date. They are feasible. And most importantly, they have that "wow" factor. For example, if you had a goal of becoming a successful painter, and told yourself that you needed to start selling artwork within a month of starting your work, you'd be setting yourself up for failure. But, if you set a target of finishing one painting at the end of your first month of work, you'd have an encouraging and exciting goal that you'd be very likely to meet.

Ask yourself these questions about your initial target:

Is your target **specific**?:

Is your target **feasible**?:

Is your target a **"wow"**?:

Does it have rational and objective measurement? Does it have an end date? Is it brief? Can I describe it succinctly?

Is it something that can be done? Can I do it?

Does it make me excited? Is it something worthwhile? Is it important to me? Is it more special than my ordinary goal or task?

WATCH

THE

W E A T H E R

Now it's time to revise your target—to make it more pointed, more achievable, and, most importantly, attuned to the external factors in the world that will inevitably hinder or enhance the probability of its success. This is when you will watch the weather.

In Western Michigan, where I grew up, the weather is wildly erratic. This is what a typical day is like in the region: at noon, it's 70 degrees and sunny, before dinner it starts raining, and by early evening, there's snow on the ground. When you live in an environment like this, you learn to adapt at a fundamental level: you don't change the weather—you work with the weather.

The same is true for innovation. When you first set your growth targets, you also need to account for the things that are happening around that target—the opportunities that are driving your target, the factors that directly and indirectly affect your target.

I call this watching the weather: being hyper-aware of what's going on around you.

Here are some things that you want to pay attention to when you're watching the weather:

- Strategic Plans

- Mission

- Business objectives

- Major projects and initiatives

- Business culture and values

- Key leaders and stakeholders

- Core organizational processes

- Current technology and methodologies

- Financials of competitors

- Publication and web information on competitors

- Annual reports

- Consumer demand and customer segment reports

- Industry analysis

The fundamental questions to ask yourself are these:

WHAT OPPORTUNITIES ARE DRIVING YOUR TARGET?

WHAT BARRIERS ARE HINDERING YOUR TARGET?

This is where the Innovation Genome comes in.

The goal is to look at the same weather through four different perspectives. You can think about a single factor from the perspective of a yellow-thinker, **blue-thinker**, **red-thinker**, and **green-thinker**.

Imagine looking out a four-pane window, with each pane a different color. When you look at the weather through each pane, you will see the same thing, but you will see it through four different lenses. If you look out the window and see a deer feeding outside your house, from a blue perspective, you might see the deer as an intruder, feeding on your rhododendrons, and conclude that the deer needs to be stopped. From the yellow perspective, you might see the deer eating the rhododendrons and reflect on how we've eliminated all their woodlands, and let them eat the plants. From the green perspective, you might brainstorm ways of doing something new or different with the deer. From the red perspective, you might think about how to control the deer, to stabilize their population so as to regulate their presence on your property.

COLLABORATE

Customers
&
Community

CREATE

Trends
&
Breakthroughs

CONTROL

Regulations
&
Standards

COMPETE

Competitors
&
Investors

Your goal is to think about the particular factors that may hinder or enhance your target from all of these perspectives.

Now, ask yourself: What is the probability that each of these things will actually happen? And, if they do happen, what kind of impact will they have on the success of your target?

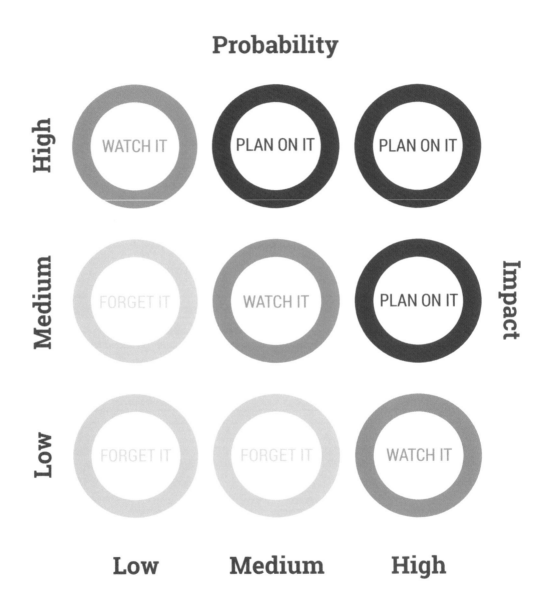

The key here is not to eliminate barriers but to build on opportunities that exist. With these factors in mind, you can restate your target so as to improve both the probability and impact of success.

CHAPTER 3

Enlist deep & diverse domain expertise

Everyone is an expert at something— and everyone is inept at something else.

This is a simple fact about the different kinds of shapes people come in. A Harvard Ph.D. candidate in Medieval History who's recently become a father could benefit from talking to a stay-at-home mother of five children. That same mother, who wants to finish her novel-in-progress, could benefit from talking to the Ph.D. candidate's good friends who work in publishing.

Innovation is a team sport. You need to assemble the group of people—the experts in areas where you alone can't deliver—who will work with you to make growth happen.

This means embracing people you may have nothing in common with: people who see the world differently than you do. This is what I mean by *enlist deep & diverse domain expertise*.

Consider, for example, my own experience working with a local news network that was having trouble keeping their ratings up. Not too long ago there was a very large shift in the way that people watch TV; so many viewers now watch by paying a fee to an Internet media provider. So it wasn't surprising when this network wasn't seeing the numbers it wanted to see. When they called me in, what I found was a room full of talented writers and newscasters, professionals with extensive credentials who truly cared about the news and bringing it to the masses.

The problem was they were simply re-trying things they had already done for years that had not worked, and they were exceptionally traditional and stubborn about changing their approach. I knew that to find an answer to their problem they would need to hire a completely different kind of expert: a young, creative, and non-traditional expert. Finally giving in, the network hired a young man who had previously worked for one of the most famous Internet providers in the world. He, in turn, hired his own team, and, in the most unconventional way possible, rented a warehouse that he covered in black paper to keep all prying eyes out.

Three weeks later this team emerged with a new product—I'll call this product "Orange." Orange was a brand-new Internet media provider that was free to the public, connected to social networking sites, and only contained thirty-second commercials. Orange offered many shows, but primarily focused on the shows that could be found on the network they were created by. Shortly after its release, it was quickly bought by the national network and is now offered in two forms: its free, original form and a fee-based, subscription form that includes full seasons of shows and movies.

Orange almost single-handedly saved this network and is now one of the two most frequently used internet media providers in the country.

What all of this tells us is: sometimes stepping out of a business's comfort zone can yield amazing results. You need to find and talk to people who do and see the things that you can't.

You need to use people who will fill in your gaps, make up for your shortcomings— whose strengths complement your weaknesses.

Teachers
Communicators
Counselors
Listeners
Conflict mediators
Community builders

Dreamers and visionaries
Fashion trend setters
Creative actors
Big picture thinkers
Experimenters
Energizers

Planners
Organizers
Analysts
Technicians and scientists
Methodical problem solvers
Professionals

Competitors
Decision makers
Goal oriented achievers
Sprinters
Political gamemasters
Dealmakers

Group think

Irrational
enthusiasm

Isolation from
external pressures

Unrealistic
vision

Poor methodology

Lack of discipline

Overreliance
on credentials

Total acceptance of facts

Right way and wrong
way of thinking

Over-emphasis
on competition

Short term focus

Autocratic decision
making

Look at the problems that come with the strengths of each quadrant. **Greens are mercurial**. They pick up every pebble on the beach. **Reds are incredibly judgmental**. They think there's a right and wrong answer for everything. **Blues think that the only way to get to anything meaningful is to fight over it**. They are relentless and cut-throat in their competitive spirit. Yellows just want to get along—often at the expense of rational reflection. They have trouble seeing and understanding external pressures.

The point is not that you can correct any of this. Rather, we need to forgive everyone for who they are and learn how to take both their strengths and their weaknesses. Every kind of person has a different way of speaking—and when we approach people who aren't like us, we need to adapt to their mode of communication. **Blues get to the point**. Yellows gather together and talk about their feelings. **Reds share data**. **Greens engage in experiments and express themselves in creative outlets**.

Talk about personal experiences Tell stories Smile Express emotion Put the person at ease Think out loud Use nonverbal gestures Acknowledge the role of intuition Recognize important spiritual symbols	Be enthusiastic and energetic Look at the big picture Expect to be interrupted in mid-sentence Draw concepts Use metaphors Look at the future Make it conceptually sound and clear Ask open-ended questions Explore how the pieces fit together
Provide details Be neat and on-time Follow the rules Explain in sequential order Conform to accepted esprit de corps Ask closed-ended questions Provide detailed data Demonstrate how it works	Go to the point and summarize Be logical and analytical Critically confront the downside Use quantifiable facts to illustrate points Be very matter-of-fact Don't get emotional Show personal ownership Demonstrate a bias towards action

What are your weaknesses? What are your blindspots? These are the kinds of people you need on your team: the people who fill in those blindspots, the people who will complement your strengths. **Ask yourself this: Who do you need on your team? And who should be your advisor?** Surround yourself with people who do not think like you, who, at a fundamental level, are completely unlike you and yet who can teach you and give you things that you cannot give yourself.

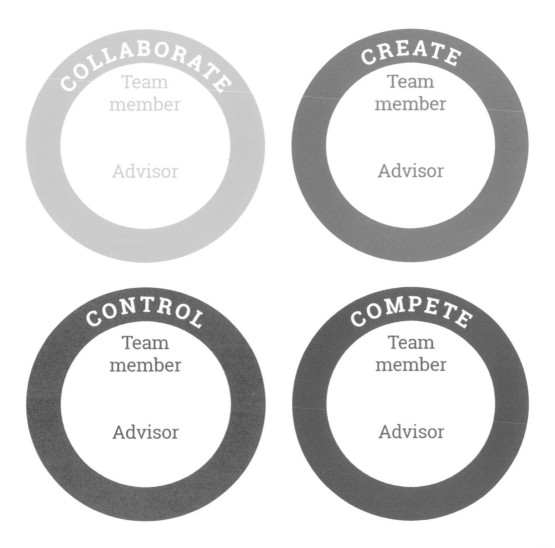

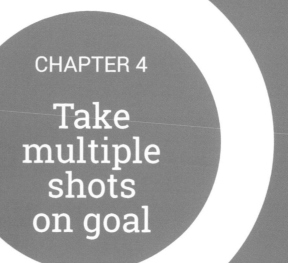

CHAPTER 4

Take multiple shots on goal

Some years back, I worked with a well-known chemical company to create an amazing new product: a fiber-optic cable that does not crack. This cable would be able to withstand excessive amounts of weight, weather, and temperatures thus revolutionizing the market.

After running a lot of experiments and taking multiple shots on goal, the company still came up short of where they wanted to be. Suddenly, a member of the company said that he had taken their product to Russia, and that so far it was receiving very good results. Russia turned out to be the perfect answer because of the notoriously harsh climate and extreme technological changes every decade or so. By using my innovation strategies of learning from experience and experiments as well as trying out their product in an emerging market, the company was able to turn a $40 million dollar profit in their first quarter from the cable. This company now boasts numbers in the billions annually and the cable is still one of their most successful and widely used products.

Here is a perfect example of the benefits of experimentation after experimentation.

Innovation is a constantly changing thing, just like the market, demand, and availability of resources. That key factor of bringing the cable to Russia changed the way they thought about growth. It was one roadblock but the company and its members saw innovation as its benefactor and experimentation as its transformation.

It's a seemingly simple concept that many people don't get:

TRY A LOT OF THINGS A LITTLE BIT.

There are too many people who make a big plan and put everything into following that plan only to find that it doesn't work out that way.

The obvious—and useful—metaphor here is an athletic one.

In any sport, the more shots you take, the more likely you are to score and the less time and energy you have to spend defending yourself, because your opponent is focused on defending themselves.

The goal here is the constant generation of new ideas and rapid experimentation.

There are four attributes I associate with this kind of dynamic thinking—what I call **structured brainstorming**.

The first is **fluency**—the ability to come up with many ideas. Whoever said one good idea is better than one hundred bad ideas was wrong. One hundred bad ideas are much better than one good idea—because out of them will come *three* good ideas. Never fall in love with the first idea you have.

The second is **flexibility**—the ability to see something in one place and apply it to another.

The third is **freedom**: don't just be open-minded but allow your mind to wander in directions you would've never looked before.

The fourth is **flow**—*energy*. It's about getting talented and vigorous people together and seeing what happens.

Consider the following sets of trigger words. These are words, phrases, ideas, thoughts to get your own thoughts going—to start this structured brainstorming experience. Once you've read through these, your mind will start to go in its own direction. Embrace this. Write down trigger words, phrases, ideas, and thoughts of your own. Identify people you know who come to mind when you hear these trigger words. What would they say? What would a red person say? A green person? A yellow person? A blue person?

TRIGGER WORDS AND PHRASES

Search and reapply best practices

Collaborate with customers

Run focus groups

Mentor and coach

Build balanced teams

Establish shared values

Hire and train lifelong learners

Develop a strong cultural identity

Create breakthrough new products

Build a strong brand

Start up a new organization

Reward strong sales

Brainstorm novel solutions

Invest in proven winners

Forecast the future

Outsource non-essential services

Enlist radicals

Maximize the value of the product portfolio

Spin off an existing unit

Improve processes

Diversify experiments

Benchmark best in class

Build a virtual organization

Remove unnecessary parts

Eliminate unprofitable products and services

Run simulations

Merge with another organization

Mine information

Pay for performance

Connect the systems

Reorganize

Work with suppliers

You'll often find that you have an interesting idea that needs to be amped up. The following are sets of questions that will help you do exactly that.

These questions will help you with an idea that just doesn't feel cool enough—an ordinary idea that's missing something extraordinary:

Combine: what if we combined this with something else?

Reverse: what if we did the opposite?

Expand: what if we did it larger?

Adapt: what if we changed some part of this?

Trim: what if we made it smaller?

Exchange: what if we traded places with something else?

These questions will help you with an idea that feels too weird—a potentially great idea that needs to be brought back down to the real world:

Credibility: how would we get stakeholders to believe we have what it takes to pursue this idea?

Resources: what money and other resources are required to pursue this idea?

Interest: what do we personally want from pursuing this idea?

Time: what are the timelines for pursuing this idea?

Information: what facts and data should we apply to this idea?

Qualifications: what expertise do we have to pursue this idea?

Understanding: what do we know about this idea?

Effect: what result will this idea produce?

Now that you have many sets of ideas, you need to identify the best ones. The best ideas have three qualities. First, they provide a real solution to the challenge at hand. Two, they are feasible. Feasible does not necessarily mean easy. Rather, it refers to something that, given your resources and constraints, you can actually achieve. Third—and most importantly—the best ideas have that "wow" factor. Wow means different things to different people. For yellows, wow is harmonious. For greens, wow is radical. For blue, wow is profitable. For red, wow is turn-key. You know an idea has that wow factor when it's something you normally wouldn't have thought of, something you couldn't have thought of on your own. Courage is a key quality here. The biggest problem is that people will often have great ideas on the board, but they'll be afraid of them. Wow can be scary. This is why you need to be fearless.

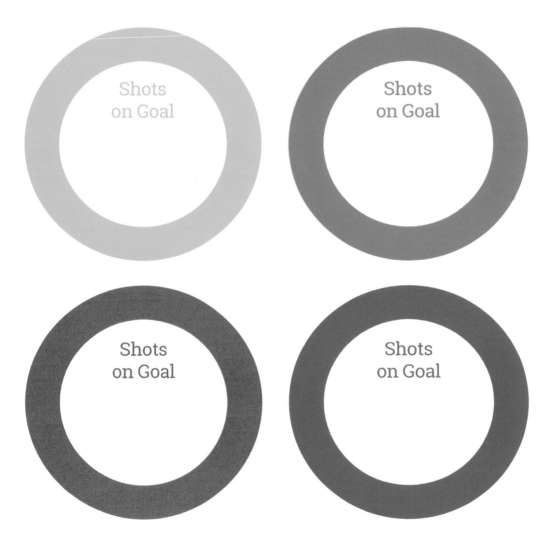

What if we took two excellent ideas from two opposite groups—a red idea and a green idea or a yellow idea and blue idea—and combined them into a new idea? This is not to ask you to bolt one idea to another. What I'm asking is much more challenging: to create a totally new idea from two old ones. How can I have the experience of reading delivered to my house? How can I communicate with my friends and everyone else in the world simultaneously?

This is being creative a second time. This is the ultimate goal. Push yourself and push others. Synthesis is where true originality happens.

CHAPTER 5

Learn from experience & experiments

THIS IS HOW AND WHERE

YOU GET SMARTER

The crucial element here is being objective about your experiments. Deconstruct your experiment. Take it apart. This is the first step in rebuilding the experiment anew. In this way, we might say that you deconstruct to reconstruct.

Think of this as running to the locker-room at halftime and making adjustments. It's not about sticking to your guns or keeping an old plan. It's about adapting to what's going on around you.

It's about paying attention to what's working—and what's not working.

Consider, for example, my experience consulting with a well-known beverage company recognized for their unrivaled marketing campaigns and consistently profitable products. This company had created a break-through artificial sweetener that tasted much closer to sugar than any other artificial sweetener on the market with absolutely no calories. Along with this sweetener, the company created an aluminum bottle, which keeps beverages colder longer and is easier to recycle than plastic. This new product—with the new sweetener, packaged in the new bottle—tasted very similar to the company's most well-known beverage.

The company tested their new product in North Africa where it did very well. However, when the product hit U.S. shelves, it bombed, due to the public's lack of understanding about its new benefits and enhancements. At this point, the company called me in to help them figure out what went wrong, how to fix it, and what their next move should be. I showed the company that what they really had on their hands were three products: the sweetener, the bottle, and the beverage.

After we sat down and examined their options, they found that the most lucrative move was to patent all three and sell them. The sweetener was packaged and marketed as a non-calorie sweetener that tastes as natural as sugar. It is now sold in stores world-wide and used by major coffee houses such as Starbucks. The bottle was licensed to beer companies, who found that it keeps their beer cold longer while reducing their packaging costs. Finally, the beverage was given a shiny new name that evokes the company's most popular product and repackaged in its original plastic bottle that America had grown to love. But it keeps the calorie-free sweetener. It is now one of the highest grossing beverages in the country.

This was all about learning from experience and experiments—seeing what worked and what didn't work and growing from those early mistakes.

Mistake	Correction
BELIEVING YOU CAN SEE THE FUTURE	MAKE SMALLER AND WIDER BETS
CHOOSING BIG OVER FAST	PICK UP YOUR PACE
MISTAKING YOUR MANAGERS FOR INNOVATORS	ENCOURAGE AND SUPPORT YOUR DEVIANTS
HAVING MORE AMBITION THAN CAPABILITY	BASE YOUR STRATEGY ON YOUR CAPABILITY
STARTING AT THE CENTER AND MOVING OUT	WORK YOUR INNOVATIONS FROM THE OUTSIDE-IN
LISTENING TO THE WRONG CUSTOMERS	FOLLOW THE CUSTOMERS THAT MOVE FIRST
FAILING TO CONNECT THE DOTS	CREATE CROSS-BOUNDARY SOLUTIONS AND SYNC UP BUSINESS MODELS

Look back on your experience and experiments. Before you identify the things that are working, identify the things that aren't working. The reason for this is a simple one: it's always easier to identify failure than it is to identify success.

We have a tendency to try to work out what isn't working. What I tell people to do is exactly the opposite:

cut your losses and build on what is working.

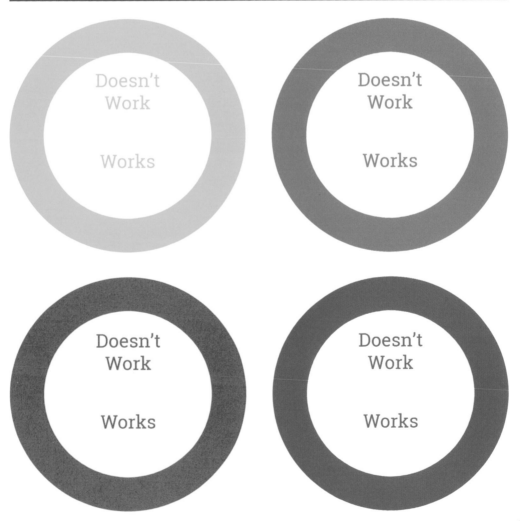

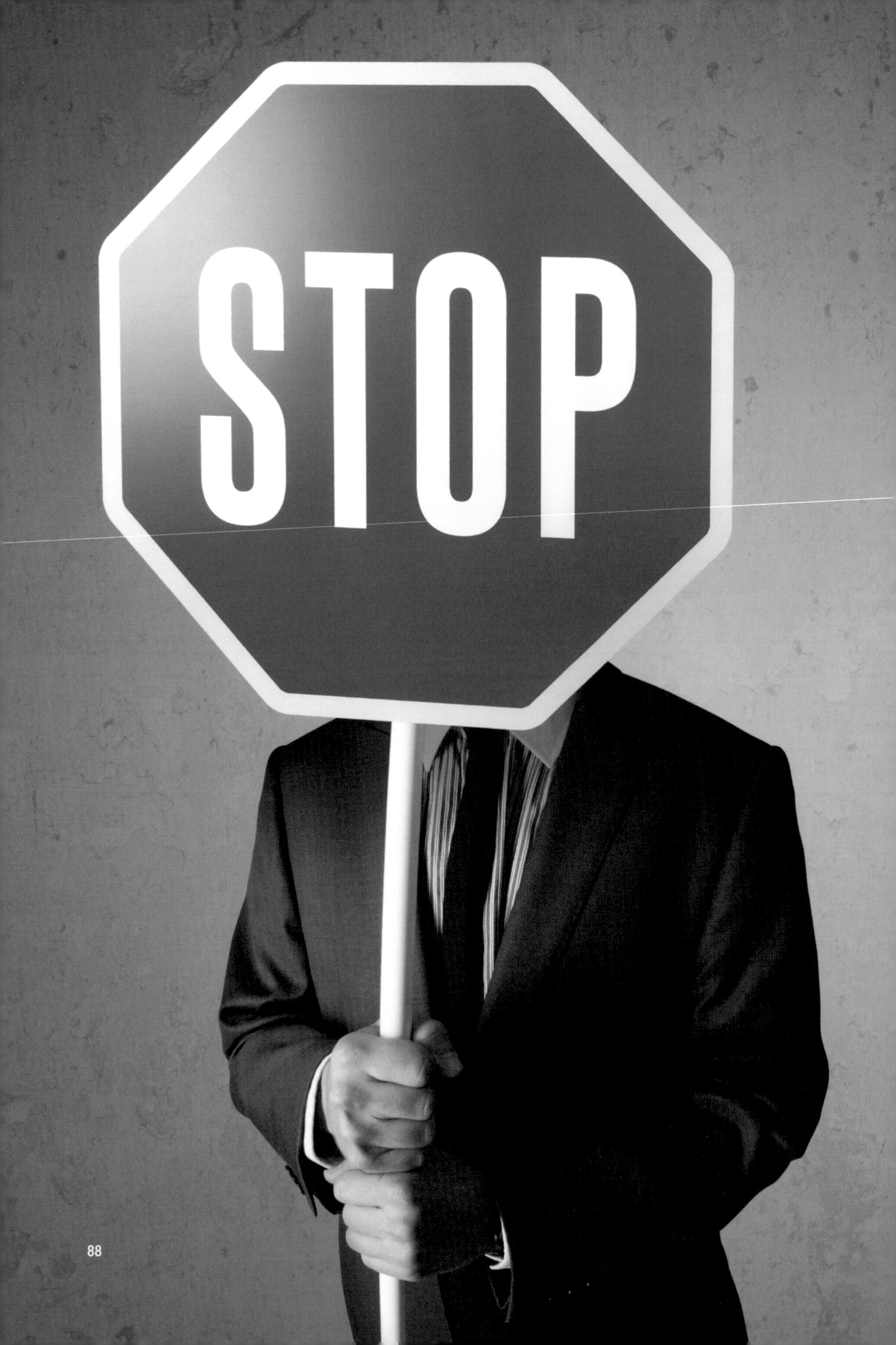
STOP

Now it's time to make your adjustments. Once you've diagnosed the things that are and aren't working, these adjustments are easy. What do you stop or do less of? What do you start or do more of? And what do you continue doing?

It makes sense to begin with what you need to stop doing. This is because stopping things is much harder than starting them. Imagine if you were to stop doing some of the things you do on a weekly basis. You decide to stop going to faculty meetings. Or you choose to stop going to mass on Sunday. Stopping has transactional costs: people get mad at you, you lose social prestige—in short, you face external consequences.

But you will never have the capacity to start unless you stop.

A lawyer who wants to write a novel needs to start working now. If she plans on waiting until she makes partner to begin writing, assuming she'll have more time, she'll miss the opportunity she has now. Of course when she makes partner, she'll have even more things to do. If she doesn't stop something that she's doing right now, she won't ever make the time to write the novel.

Start/Do More

Stop/Do Less

Stay/Do Nothing

Start/Do More

Stop/Do Less

Stay/Do Nothing

Start/Do More

Stop/Do Less

Stay/Do Nothing

Start/Do More

Stop/Do Less

Stay/Do Nothing

This is when you re-start the cycle. Now that you've made your adjustments and learned from your experiments, it's time to start the new ones. And you do that by going back to the beginning: state and re-state your new high-quality targets. Review, revise, and repeat.

Innovation is merely connecting the dots. This is exactly what I mean when I say making stone soup: bringing together people with diverse talents and worldviews—reds and greens, yellows and blues—and connecting them with each other, creating something special out of these disparate ingredients.

But once you've hit your innovation sweet spot, the work has only just begun. Innovation is a cyclical process—it's continual. You start it, you tweak it, and you start it again. To keep innovation going, you'll need to perpetually prepare your future leaders. Think of it this way: see one, do one, teach one. Once you've mastered the skills of organic growth, show others around you. By developing a community of highly practiced innovation leaders, you create a mentor system that ensures that the cycle of innovation will continue. Today's leaders transfer deep knowledge about the art of innovation to those who will become future leaders, all while working on projects with high potential for developing new practices and competencies.

Innovation is a skill acquired only through developmental learning. It's like a foreign language or a musical instrument: you've got to practice and fail before you get better. Embrace your early mistakes. Innovators are flexible—and they find opportunities in both their setbacks and their successes. Remember that you can never predict what the future will be like. Rather, you need to be prepared to adapt as things happen. Expect the unexpected: leave room for the stuff you don't know now.

LEAVE ROOM FOR THE STUFF YOU DON'T KNOW NOW

EXTRA
RESOURCES

Take the assessment:
http://innv.at/O-Assess

Watch a video of how Jeff works with the Detroit
Symphony Orchestra to make stone soup:
http://innv.at/JS-DSO

To find out more about Jeff's workshops, speaking
engagements, coaching programs, and assessment
services, visit:
http://jeffdegraff.com/

Follow Jeff on LinkedIn:
http://www.linkedin.com/influencer/degraffjeff

CPSIA information can be obtained
at www.ICGtesting.com
Printed in the USA
LVIC06n0225080115
421974LV00003B/8

9 780692 242704